The Mystery of the Spy's Diary

By Charles Higgins and Regina Higgins
Illustrated by Thea Kliros

Modern Curriculum Press
Parsippany, New Jersey

Cover and book design by John Maddalone

ISBN 0-7652-2155-1

Printed in the United States of America

6 7 8 9 10   07 06 05 04

Modern Curriculum Press

Pearson Learning Group

1-800-321-3106
www.pearsonlearning.com

CONTENTS

For Frances and Charles,
master spies

A Mystery in the Mail

The October day was sunny and cool. Karen Harper and her friends, Luke Williams, Wendy Asato, and Steve Alvarez, were walking home from school. A light wind pulled leaves from the trees and swirled them around.

Suddenly one leaf landed softly on Karen's head. She looked up just as a gust of wind blew the leaf up and away.

"What a great day!" Karen said. "If only I knew what I was doing for my history project."

"You don't have an idea yet?" Luke asked.

"No, the idea I had was already taken by the time I talked to Mrs. Delgado," Karen said.

"There isn't much time left," Wendy said. "You always hand in everything early, too. What are you going to do?"

"I don't know," Karen sighed. "We're supposed to do our reports on local history, but I can't think of anything unusual enough. I don't want to do the same old things."

"Maybe your dad could help you. He must know a lot about River City history. He's the head librarian at the River City Library," said Steve. "If he doesn't know, who does?"

As they talked, they turned a corner onto the street where Karen lived. They saw a mail truck parked outside of Karen's house. "I wonder what we're getting," Karen said.

"Let's go see," Wendy said. "I'll race you!"

The friends all ran to the house. As they ran up the front steps, Karen's dogs, Tip and Top, greeted them with happy barks and wagging tails. Inside the house, Karen's mother was just opening a small cardboard box.

"Who's it from, Mom?" Karen asked.

"It's from Aunt Emma," Karen's mother replied, reading the note. "She was cleaning out her attic and found something she thought you and your dad might be interested in. She says that it's very old."

As the friends gathered around the table, Karen looked in the box. Inside she found a book with a black cover. She took it out of the box.

"What is it?" Wendy asked.

Karen opened the book. When she turned the pages, she saw spidery writing in faded blue ink.

"I think it's a diary," Karen said. "Look, there's a date on this page. Wow, it says 1777!"

Everyone was quiet. Then Luke said, "That's when the Americans were fighting the British for their freedom in the Revolutionary War!"

"Who wrote it?" Wendy asked.

Karen turned to the first page of the book. "It says, *Property of Jacob Harper.*"

Karen's mother nodded. "Jacob Harper is an ancestor of ours. Aunt Emma told me about him. He lived during the time of the American Revolution," she said.

"That was a long time ago," Steve said.

Karen turned to another page. She studied the old-fashioned writing awhile, then tried to read it aloud. *"Today I rode to River City again. The town is growing fast."* Karen looked up. "Does he mean our River City?" she asked her mother, looking surprised.

"Maybe so," her mother replied. "The Harper family lived near here during that time."

Karen read on, *"I made sure my secret was safe in its hiding place."*

"What secret? What hiding place?" Luke, Steve, and Wendy said at the same time.

Karen turned the yellowed pages, stopping to read a few paragraphs. "He keeps calling it his secret. *My secret is safe,* he says."

Karen continued to flip the pages, then stopped again. "Listen to this," she said. "*I hope someone in my own family will find my secret one day, a long time from now. That person will need to follow the clues to solve the puzzle I have made to hide my secret.*"

"You like puzzles," Steve said to Karen. "You love history, too."

"What do you think his secret was?" Wendy asked curiously.

"I'll bet it had something to do with the Revolutionary War," Luke said.

Karen read again. "*The one who finds my secret will find a true treasure.*"

"A treasure!" Steve nearly shouted.

"What did Jacob Harper do?" Luke asked. "Was he a farmer?"

Karen turned a page and read to herself. Then she looked up slowly, her eyes wide. "He was a spy!" she said.

Clues and Riddles

Karen turned the diary around to show the other kids. She pointed to the top of a page and read aloud, *"I am a man of secrets, a spy."*

"Your ancestor was a spy in the Revolutionary War!" Steve said excitedly.

"He left a secret treasure here in River City!" Wendy added.

"What about the clues?" asked Luke. "Are they in the diary, too?"

Luke, Steve, and Wendy crowded in by Karen as she looked through the old book.

"I didn't know they had spies then," Steve said as Karen carefully turned the pages.

"Spies have been around for a long time, even before the Revolutionary War," Mrs. Harper explained. "Each side in a war wants to find out what the enemy is planning. Spies get the information and send back secret messages."

"In those days, they didn't have telephones or e-mail," Steve said. "It must have been hard to send secret messages."

Mrs. Harper smiled. "Before computers, spies sent messages on paper. A spy would write his message in code so that only another person who knew the code could read it," she said.

"I know about codes," Steve replied. "My grandfather leaves me notes in code, just for fun. He uses numbers instead of letters—1 is A, 2 is B, and so on."

"Codes are fun," agreed Mrs. Harper, "but in a war a coded message would be very serious. It might tell about plans for a battle. If he really was a spy during the Revolutionary War, Jacob Harper's secrets were probably very important. They were also probably very dangerous."

"Why?" asked Wendy.

"An army wouldn't want the enemy finding out where, when, or how they planned to attack. They would be careful to guard their plans. If they found someone trying to steal their secrets, they would probably capture the person," Mrs. Harper said. "They might even kill him!"

Karen suddenly called, "Here's a clue!" She read, *"The key that unlocks the secret lies in the darkness below the darkness."* She looked up at her friends. "What does that mean?"

"It sounds like a riddle," said Steve, shaking his head.

"I don't understand," Wendy said, frowning. "What could that mean?"

"What else does he say?" Luke asked, reaching for the diary. He pointed to the next page. *"Follow the river to the Post Road Bridge. Between the bridge and the schoolhouse, there is a sundial,"* he read.

"What is the Post Road Bridge?" Steve wanted to know.

"Some of the landmarks Jacob Harper tells about are probably gone by now," Mrs. Harper told him. "The bridge and the schoolhouse may have been torn down."

"The river is still there," said Wendy.

"What is a sundial?" asked Luke.

"I know!" Wendy cried. "It's a clock that uses sunlight and shadow to tell the time. I made one last year for science class." Then she frowned and said, "I don't know where there are any sundials in River City, though."

"There must have been one here at the time of the Revolutionary War," Luke replied. "Maybe it's gone now, too."

"Then how can we find the secret treasure?" asked Steve.

"Maybe we can find out where the sundial used to be," Karen said. She picked up the book again and read. "*At one o'clock, stand where the shadow ends. Walk northwest one hundred steps, and look for the bird that will never fly.*"

"We can find northwest with the compass I use when I go hiking," Steve said. "What about the bird that will never fly?"

"It's another riddle," Luke sighed.

"Jacob Harper must have liked riddles," Mrs. Harper said, laughing, "just as you do." She hugged Karen.

Karen smiled at her mother. "I'm going to find his secret treasure, Mom. I think I'm the family member who is meant to find it." Everyone knew that when Karen decided to do something, she would keep trying until she got it done.

"We'll help you!" cried Steve.

Luke agreed. "All we have to do is follow the clues and solve the riddles!"

Wendy jumped up. "Let's go right now!"

"Wait a minute!" Mrs. Harper raised her hands. "You have to decide where to look first, and you shouldn't go without an adult. Besides, it's getting dark. These fall days end early, you know."

The friends looked out the window. The sun was already beginning to set, and the shadows were growing longer.

Karen sighed. "Well, I guess Jacob Harper's secret can wait until tomorrow. I have to think of something for my history project anyway."

Just then a folded piece of paper slipped out of the diary. Karen picked it up. "What is this?" she asked as she carefully unfolded it.

"Is it another clue?" asked Luke.

Karen shook her head as she looked at the paper. "I don't think so," she said. "It looks funny, and it doesn't make sense."

She turned the page around so that her friends could see the writing.

"It's in a secret code!" Steve whispered.

What Now?

The next afternoon after school, Steve was helping Luke rake leaves. Karen had already finished raking leaves in her yard, so she and Wendy took a walk near River City Park. They talked about the diary and the secret treasure.

"Did you find any more clues in Jacob Harper's diary?" Wendy asked. "What about that secret message in code?"

Karen shook her head. "I read the whole diary, and I still don't know any more about the secret or that message. Mom and Dad couldn't figure it out either."

"If we found the secret," Wendy said, "maybe we'd know what the coded message means."

"Maybe," Karen replied. "There's nothing about the code in the diary."

"What did Jacob Harper write about in his diary?" Wendy asked.

"He wrote a lot about his everyday life," Karen told her. "He used to make chairs and soap and candles. I guess people had to do a lot of things themselves long ago."

Wendy stopped to pick up a small, sparkly stone. "I'd like to read the diary sometime," Wendy said as she examined the stone.

"Sure," Karen said, smiling. She knew how much Wendy liked making things. "Jacob tells all about the way he makes candles. I love reading about how people lived a long time ago, especially when it's someone I'm related to."

The girls stood and watched children playing in the playground. Many things they saw reminded them of the clues and the riddles that might lead to a secret treasure. The shadows of trees on the ground made them think about sundials. As they watched a bird fly over the river, they thought about a bird that would never fly.

"Penguins can't fly," Wendy pointed out. "Chickens can't fly very well."

"Penguins don't live around here," said Karen. "It can't be a real bird, anyway. A live bird wouldn't be around after two hundred years." She sighed. "He must mean something else."

The friends sat down on the grassy slope. They looked out over the river. Far away they could see the tops of houses and the tall buildings downtown.

"River City must have changed a lot in over two hundred years," Karen said. "Jacob Harper probably never saw most of those buildings across the river."

"Some things have stayed the same," Wendy said. "The river and those caves up there in the hills are the same," she said. She pointed toward some nearby hills. "They've been here forever. Jacob Harper would have known about them."

Karen counted the mysterious landmarks on her fingers. "He wrote about the Post Road Bridge, the schoolhouse, and the sundial."

"Where could they be?" Wendy asked.

Karen sighed. "Like Mom said, they may not even be around anymore."

Wendy thought for a minute. "The diary says to follow the river to the Post Road Bridge. Let's follow the river now! That might give us a start."

Karen shook her head. "I told my parents I wouldn't go looking for these places alone. It's getting late anyway."

Wendy looked out to the hills. "If only we could see River City as Jacob Harper saw it over two hundred years ago."

Suddenly Karen jumped up. "That's it, Wendy!" she shouted. "Let's go!" Karen turned and ran to the sidewalk.

"Where are you going?" called Wendy, running after her.

Karen stopped, breathless. "We're going to see River City the way Jacob Harper saw it. Then we'll know where to look for the secret treasure. Come on! Let's go ask your mom if she can give us a ride. Then we'll go get Steve and Luke!"

A Look Into the Past

At the River City Library, Karen, Wendy, Luke, and Steve got out of Mrs. Asato's car and quickly climbed the steps.

"Why are we going to the library?" asked Luke. "How will this help us find the secret treasure?"

"Karen said we would see River City the way Jacob Harper saw it," Wendy told him. "Karen is going to ask her dad to help us."

Inside they went directly to a room with a sign over the door. The sign said, Local History Research Room.

"What is this place?" asked Steve.

"This is where we can find out facts about River City a long time ago," Karen told him.

Inside they found Karen's dad. She told him what they were looking for. He went over to a shelf and took down a big roll of paper. He spread it out on a table.

"Here's something you should see," Mr. Harper said as he smoothed out the paper.

"What is it?" asked Steve. "It looks like a treasure map."

Mr. Harper laughed. "In a way it is. For people interested in history, this map is a kind of treasure just waiting to be found and read."

The friends gathered around the paper. Luke read the words at the top: *River City, 1790.*

Steve's eyes got wider as he realized what they were looking at. "This map shows River City the way it was when Jacob Harper lived here!"

"Almost," Mr. Harper added. "The map was made 13 years after Jacob Harper wrote the diary. Some things probably have changed, but you may be able to find some of the landmarks he talks about in the diary."

The friends looked closely at the carefully drawn map of their town. Karen saw that the downtown area had only two streets. A few farms were marked, and a road was shown winding near the town.

Karen sighed. "How do we know where anything is? It's like a different town."

Wendy traced a blue line through the map. "The river is the same," she said.

"The river is a good landmark," Mr. Harper agreed. "Look, here's another help, a compass rose." He pointed to a design on the map. It looked a little like a flower with four points sticking out of it. A letter—N, E, S, W—was above each point.

"That should tell us where north is on the map," Steve said.

Karen looked again. "So this road," she traced it lightly with a finger, "runs north of the river and the town."

Mr. Harper looked closely at the map. "It's called the Post Road. That would be the main road in and out of town. The coaches and the mail wagons that delivered the post used it. That's how it got its name."

"Where it crosses the river would be the Post Road Bridge!" cried Karen. "There it is!"

"Do you need anything else?" Mr. Harper asked.

Karen thought for a minute. "We need to find the schoolhouse and the sundial." The friends searched the map. They found the schoolhouse on a hill north of the river, but no sundial.

Luke sighed. "I guess we're out of luck."

"No, we're not," Karen told him. "We have three landmarks. Maybe we'll find the sundial when we try to follow the Post Road."

"I've never seen a Post Road, except on this map," said Wendy. "How will we find it for real?"

"We know it's north of town," Steve pointed out, "and then it crosses the river. Maybe my grandfather can help us find it. He knows lots of old paths around town."

"That's great!" said Karen. "Let's meet at Wendy's house Saturday morning. Will you come with us, Dad?"

Mr. Harper nodded, smiling. "I don't have to work this weekend. I think your mother will want to be in on the fun, too," he said.

Karen felt like shouting for joy. She was sure they were going to solve Jacob Harper's riddles and find his secret treasure!

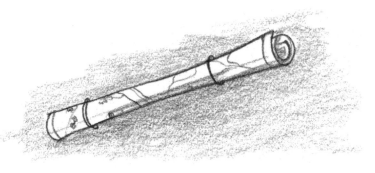

CHAPTER 5

The Post Road Bridge

Early Saturday morning, Karen, Steve, and Luke went to Wendy's house. With them were Mr. and Mrs. Harper and Mr. Alvarez, Steve's grandfather.

Mr. Harper brought a copy he had made of the town map from the library. Carefully, he taped it on the wall so that everyone could see it.

Karen pointed to the map. "Here's the Post Road that Jacob Harper wrote about in his diary. If we can find it, we'll be able to get closer to the secret treasure," she said.

"We know it's north of town, and that it crosses the river over here," added Luke.

Mr. Alvarez thought for a minute. Then he stepped up to the map. "I've taken walks in this area. The trees and bushes are thick, but there is a path."

The friends jumped up, excited to go at once.

After everyone had gotten into the Harpers'
van, they drove down to the river and found a
spot to park. The sun was shining warmly as they
hiked through the tall grass. Steve led the way
with his grandfather.

Suddenly Mr. Alvarez stopped. "Beyond these
oak trees, we'll come to a path. It might be
what's left of the road we're looking for," he said.

Karen, Steve, Luke, and Wendy ran ahead until
they came to a clearing among the trees.

"Where is it?" asked Luke.

"Look down!" Mr. Alvarez said. Beneath their
feet there was a narrow dirt path.

"Is this the Post Road?" asked Steve. "It sure
doesn't look like a road."

"There's only one way to find out," said Karen.
"Let's follow it."

The friends started walking down the path while the others followed closely. The tall trees blocked the sunlight, and a chilly breeze began to blow. They walked for over an hour, until Karen wondered if they should turn back.

Then they heard Steve yell in pain. "There's something here. I just tripped over it," he called.

Karen, Wendy, and Luke rushed forward into another little clearing. They found themselves near the river. Steve was rubbing his leg and pointing to stones that looked like the remains of a short column.

"What is this?" Karen asked.

Mr. Harper examined the stones. "There's another one over there," he said, pointing to the remains of a second stone column.

"Look," Mrs. Harper added, pointing to a date carved in one stone.

"Wow! 1772!" cried Luke. "What is this?"

"These stones could be supports for an old wooden bridge," Mr. Alvarez said. "This point is where the river is narrowest. We might find more of these stones on the other side of the river."

"This must be the Post Road Bridge," Wendy said. Then she whirled around. "Where's the sundial? It should be nearby."

"It might be on the other side of the river," Mr. Harper said. "The diary didn't say exactly where it would be."

"The diary said it was between the bridge and the schoolhouse," Karen said. "So let's see if we can find the schoolhouse."

The group turned around and walked through the tall grass. They saw the hills in the distance, and they could just make out the caves near the top, but they found no schoolhouse.

Karen sighed. "We've come so far. It looks as if we'll never find what we're looking for."

"Remember, Karen," Mr. Alvarez said, "the schoolhouse was just a landmark, so maybe we could find the sundial without the schoolhouse."

"Even if the building is not here anymore, maybe we could find old ruins or some sign where it may have been," Steve said. "Let's split up and look!"

Everyone looked down and began walking
slowly, searching for the sundial. Karen stared at
the ground, trying to see what might be beneath
the grass. She moved toward an oak tree, her
feet crunching on the brown leaves spread over
the ground. Suddenly she thought she saw
something. She knelt down and pushed aside the
dry leaves, but nothing was there.

When she looked up, she saw a pair of hiking
boots among the leaves. She jumped up in
surprise. A man with white hair was standing in
front of her, and he looked angry.

CHAPTER 6

A Friend Shows the Way

"What are you doing here?" the man said.

Karen gasped and turned to run. Suddenly her father was behind her.

"We're sorry," Mr. Harper said. "We didn't mean to trespass. Is this your land?"

"Yes, it is," the man replied. He looked a little less angry. "I don't like kids wandering around here. They could get hurt."

Karen spoke up. "My name is Karen Harper," she said. "This is my mom and dad. We're looking for something we read about in my ancestor's diary."

"Well, I'm Robert Connor," the man said, shaking hands with Karen, her parents, and Mr. Alvarez. "I'm sorry if I sounded like a big grouch, but I worry about kids getting into trouble in the woods and up in those caves."

"You're right about that," Mrs. Harper said. "That's why we came along."

Mr. Connor folded his arms and looked right at Karen. "You said something about an ancestor's diary? I'd like to hear about it. History is my hobby, especially local history."

Karen told Mr. Connor about Jacob Harper's diary and the secret treasure.

Mr. Connor smiled. "What a great story!" he said. "You may not have much luck though. River City has changed a lot in two hundred years."

"We know!" sighed Luke. "We've been trying to find the landmarks Jacob Harper wrote about. We found where the Post Road Bridge was, but not much else."

Mr. Connor laughed. "Well, local history can be tricky. You've done a good job so far. Old maps and diaries can help."

"We're stuck now," Karen said. "We have to find a sundial."

"A sundial?" Mr. Connor asked. "I've never heard of a sundial around here. Where does the diary say it was?"

"The diary said it's between the Post Road Bridge," Karen pointed, "and a schoolhouse. We found the schoolhouse on the map, but we haven't been able to see it anywhere here."

"The schoolhouse!" Mr. Connor exclaimed.

"Do you know it?" asked Karen.

"I hope so," Mr. Connor said laughing. "I bought the old schoolhouse about forty years ago and fixed it up. It's my house now. I live there!"

Mr. Connor pointed to a small white house on the top of a nearby hill. The kids' faces brightened.

"Then the sundial must be right around here!" cried Karen, turning around. "Will you help us look?" she asked Mr. Connor.

"Sure!" he said. "If the sundial was part of the schoolhouse property, it's got to be somewhere around here. I've probably walked over it a million times without knowing it!"

They started looking again. They walked back and forth across the clearing and up and down the hill. From time to time, Karen gently pushed back the branches of a bush to see the ground.

The sun was beginning to set. Karen rubbed her hands together to warm them. Her dad walked over and said they should think about going home. They could try again tomorrow.

Suddenly Mr. Connor shouted, "Over here!"

Everyone ran to Mr. Connor. He was on his knees looking at a patch of grass. "See here?" he asked. "What do you make of that?"

Karen looked closely at the ground. Mr. Connor had swept away a thin layer of dirt. There was a dull, silvery glow peeking through the dirt. Karen got on her knees and gently brushed away more of the dirt.

"What is it, Karen?" asked Steve.

Karen worked a little longer, then stood up to show what she had found. It was a picture of a shining sun.

The Cave

"It's the sundial!" Luke cried. Everyone looked at it, amazed that they had actually found it.

"I can't believe it's been here all this time and I never saw it," Mr. Connor said, shaking his head.

"Well, that's about it for today," Mrs. Harper said. "We've got to get back to the car before it gets any darker. Mr. Connor, thank you so much for helping us. May we come back tomorrow and continue our search?"

"Yes," Mr. Connor said. "This is the most fun I've had in a long time."

The next day the kids returned to the same spot with Mr. and Mrs. Harper and Mr. Alvarez. They found Mr. Connor clearing away the last of the dirt from around the sundial with a small shovel.

"I came out here as soon it was light," he told them, as he rose from his knees. "Isn't this sundial something?"

Karen looked down at the sundial in wonder. Its metal face was just like a regular clock, with carved markings around the edges to mark the hours. Over the years the metal must have worn away making the numbers hard to read. The metal pointer still stood at the center making a shadow to show the time.

"Does it still work?" Luke asked.

"It should," Mr. Connor said. "There are no moving parts. It just needs the sun."

"Well," Luke said, "I guess we don't have to wind it up again!" Everyone laughed. Luke was always making jokes.

They waited for one o'clock, when the shadow would point the way toward the secret treasure. Mr. Connor talked about River City's history. Long ago, he told them, many free Africans in the colonies settled near River City and raised their families. During the Revolutionary War, the men joined the fight for the new country's freedom.

"Jacob Harper wrote in his diary that he was a spy," Karen told Mr. Connor. She showed him the page in the diary and the piece of paper with the message in code.

"Well, what do you know?" whispered Mr. Connor. "Anything he hid would be a real treasure for the whole town."

After talking and looking at the diary to pass the time, it was finally almost one o'clock. Everyone gathered around the sundial. Slowly the shadow moved to point to one of the markings. Steve got out his compass.

Karen opened the diary to the page that talked about the sundial. "Steve, stand where the shadow ends," she said.

Steve moved his feet to touch the line where the shadow and the sunlight met. "Now walk one hundred steps northwest," Karen read.

Steve looked at his compass. "Northwest is that way," he pointed. He walked slowly as he counted. Everyone followed him.

"Ninety-eight, ninety-nine, one hundred!" Steve called. He was standing near several large rocks. "What's next?" he asked.

Karen looked at the diary again. "We've got to find the bird that will never fly."

"What is that?" asked Mr. Connor.

Luke sighed. "We don't know. It's one of Jacob Harper's riddles, and it's the hardest."

Everyone searched the grass and bushes for a clue. Steve climbed the rocks for a better look around. Mr. Alvarez sat down on a rock. He ran his hand over its smooth side. Suddenly he stopped.

"Look!" Mr. Alvarez called. "The part of the rock I've got my hand on is like a bird's wing."

Karen ran over. "I don't see it," she said,
looking at the rock. She turned her head. It still
looked like just a rock.

"You can see it if you stand back," Luke said.

Karen moved to where Luke was standing. She
stared at the rock again. "You're right!" she
cried. "It must be the bird that will never fly!"

"You found it, Papa Tito!" Steve shouted.

Mr. Alvarez raised his hand. "*We* found it, Steve. If I hadn't gotten so tired following you around, I never would have sat down."

Karen opened the diary again. "*To find my secret,*" she read aloud, "*look above the bird.*" Everyone looked up at the hills.

"It must be in that cave!" Karen cried. A dark opening in the rocks showed a cave directly above them. She and the other kids started running up the hill.

"Wait for us!" Mrs. Harper called. "Don't go in that cave by yourselves!"

The kids waited for the others at the entrance to the small cave. Then everyone went in together. The front of the cave was lit by sunlight, but the back was dim. Steve pulled out a small flashlight from his pocket. He clicked it on and moved it around the cave walls.

"Just one more clue," Karen said. "I know it by heart. *The key that unlocks the secret lies in the darkness below the darkness.*"

She thought and thought. "I can't think what the answer is," she sighed. She stood silently and looked around.

"It was pretty dark in here before I turned on my flashlight," Steve pointed out.

"The darkness could be the cave," Karen whispered. "What is the darkness below the darkness?" She looked down at the black dirt. "I've got it!" she cried. "It's the dirt! That's the darkness below the darkness, but how will we know where to dig?"

Steve continued to move his flashlight around the cave. Then he stopped. "Look!" he said. "What's that mark on the wall?"

The kids leaned close to look. Scratched into the rock was a letter "H." "Maybe H stands for Harper," Karen said. "The treasure might be buried here."

Mr. Connor handed Karen his small shovel. She dug in the soft earth, her friends gathered closely around her. Suddenly the shovel hit something hard. Karen reached into the hole and lifted out a metal box. She brushed the dirt off the top, then gently opened the lid.

"What is it, Karen?" asked Luke.

Mr. Connor looked over Karen's shoulder. "History," he whispered.

Jacob Harper's Treasure

Mr. Connor was right. The box that Jacob Harper buried in the cave was full of history. It was a real spy's kit from the Revolutionary War!

Karen held the tin box carefully on the ride back to her house. In the kitchen she spread newspaper on the table. Then she opened the box again and gently took out what was inside.

"Look at this!" she cried, holding up two small bottles and a gold ring. "What are these?"

"One of those bottles is probably invisible ink," her father said. "Long ago, spies sometimes wrote messages in ink that no one could see. That was one way they kept their messages secret."

Luke looked at the other bottle. "Is that the stuff that will make the message appear again?" he asked.

Mr. Connor nodded. "The person who got the message would put that stuff on the letter in order to read it. Spies would also mark their letters with a signet ring," he said as he pointed to the heavy gold ring Karen was holding. "There's a special design on that ring that Jacob Harper would press into warm candle wax to seal a letter."

Karen looked closely at the ring. "It's a picture of a star," she said.

"That was his sign then," Mr. Connor said. "Anyone who received a letter marked with a star knew it was from Jacob Harper."

Mr. Harper looked in the box. "There's a book at the bottom," he said.

Karen lifted the book out of the box. She opened it and found strange writing. There was a line of 26 symbols. Below each symbol was a letter. "Another riddle," Karen sighed.

"No," Steve said. "It's not a riddle, it's the answer. That's Jacob Harper's code book!"

"A code book!" Luke said. "Now we'll know what that message means!"

Mrs. Harper got Karen a sheet of paper and a pencil. Karen spread out the message that had fallen out of the diary and opened the code book. "That's T, O—To!" she whispered. She wrote the word on the sheet of paper and continued. "It's a letter to General George Washington!"

Karen carefully decoded the message letter by letter. As she worked, her father and Mr. Connor talked quietly. Then Mr. Harper went to the phone and made a call.

"I've got it!" cried Karen.

Everyone gathered around. Karen stood and held the sheet of paper before her. Then she read aloud. "*To General George Washington: Dear General, I write to tell you about recent plans I have heard from the British to attack from the Hudson River near Kingston.*"

"That's in New York!" cried Luke.

Karen read on. The letter told about a British plan to sail up the Hudson River and cut off supply lines going north to the patriots.

"I wonder if Jacob's letter did any good," Steve said.

Karen picked up the code book again. In the back of the book, she found an envelope tucked between two pages. Written on the envelope in Jacob Harper's handwriting were the words, "*My treasure.*" Karen opened the envelope and read the letter inside, "*To Jacob Harper, I write to return your note and send my thanks for your brave actions in our fight for independence. Your secret part in our plans has helped to win our freedom. We were able to stop the British before they reached Kingston.*" Karen looked up, her eyes wide. "It's signed General George Washington!"

"Jacob Harper was a hero!" Steve said.

Karen's parents hugged her while Mr. Connor and Mr. Alvarez cheered and clapped. "This is a great day for your family, Karen," Mr. Connor said, "and for River City, too!"

Mr. Harper nodded. "Mr. Connor is going to help me set up a display in the library for the spy kit, the diary, and the letter. When people find out about this, River City will be famous!"

Suddenly there was a knock on the door. "People are going to find out sooner than you think," said Mrs. Harper laughing. "The local TV news is already here. Your dad called them. They want to talk to you, Karen!"

"We're going to be on TV!" the friends cried as the reporter and the cameraperson moved in to hear their story.

After the newspeople had left, Karen sat on the sofa. She was very tired. "Now I have to get started on that history project," she said. "I still don't have a good idea."

"Yes, you do," Wendy, Luke, and Steve said almost at the same time. "You can do a report on Jacob Harper, Revolutionary War spy."

Karen looked surprised. "You're right," she cried. "Jacob Harper, you're my hero." Everyone laughed.

Glossary

ancestor (AN ses tur) a person who comes before one in a family, such as a great-great-grandparent

attic (AT ihk) a room or space just below the roof of a house

code (kohd) a kind of secret writing in which letters, numbers, or symbols stand for something else, such as letters or words

colonies (KAHL uh neez) lands that are settled and then ruled by a country some distance away

column (KAHL um) a long upright support that holds up something such as a roof or a bridge

compass (KUM pus) an instrument for showing direction

diary (DYE uh ree) a record written day by day, usually in a book, of things done, seen, or thought by the writer

landmarks (LAND mahrk) objects that are easily seen, such as a tree, building, or hill, and can be used to find or mark a certain place

patriots (PAY tree uts) people who show great love and loyalty for their country

ruins (ROO ihnz) what remains of a building or a city after it is destroyed